THE MYSTERY OF CASTLE STUART

by

John Cameron

First Written March 1930

Introduction by Charles Stuart

Published by Castle Creations Limited

Illustrations by Hugh Kirkwood, Invergordon

Dear Reader

The ebbing tide of my life compels me to take pen in hand and present for your scrutiny the strange circumstances surrounding the ancestral seat of the "Unlucky House of Stuart"; my home in the highlands of Scotland.

Castle Stuart stands today as it was created in the year of our Lord 1625; repelling unwanted guests through generations. Weathered by violent storms borne in the cruel North Sea, and battered by incessant winds which break upon its threshold; it offers no refuge to the uninvited.

One of the oldest dwellings in that part of the country it stands desolate within sight of the Moray Firth and some five miles from the town of Inverness. No longer is it occupied, or should I say tenanted ... but if you should ask any of the local folk they will hasten to tell you that "there is no peace in that house" and therein hangs this tale.

Charles Stuart,
Inverness,
December 1996

When I first laid eyes on Castle Stuart I was overcome with a rare and pleasing sense of harmony, which promised nothing but satisfaction from its further acquaintance. I had therefore no hesitation in embarking upon the solemn promise which I had made some years before to restore this ancient fortress to its former glory. Had I known then the consequence of my resolve, I would have returned to my native Canada for ever; and without a backward glance. But that was not to be and the work began.

The first months were uneventful, being happily spent in planning the campaign before turning a stone. The rudimentary plumbing and lack of electricity would present a fascinating challenge and the ruinous devastation of the Great Hall would provide years of satisfaction in its reconstruction. But above all, the restoration of the collapsed East Wing promised to become the ultimate achievement in this vast project.

Legend has it that in the winter of 1798 a storm of incredible ferocity struck the North East coast, washed out to God knows where the fishing village of Lochmarden and all of its inhabitants; lashed and laid bare the whole of the Black Isle, then roared up the Moray Firth, pounded the Castle and tore the roof off the East Tower. The damage was so severe that repairs were not even contemplated, instead, the main body of the house was sealed off from its "broken wing". And so it remained for almost 300 years until that fateful night when I broke the seal in the wall above the Great Hall.

It happened that one of my workers had that day built a makeshift ladder to examine some of the roof beams, and as it had become my custom to survey the day's work when they had gone, I decided to examine more closely an area in the wall above the Great Hall which had intrigued me from the start. The plaster coating seemed to differ from the rest and although barely visible above the naked beams it gave promise of being the opening which had been sealed off after the Great Storm.

The ladder reached only to the level of the beams but as they were sound I had no hesitation in clambering up and over them to stand erect and face what indeed appeared to be a sealed doorway. The thrill of discovery was soon tempered however by my precarious situation, yet curiosity overcame my caution and I laid to with hammer and chisel upon the yielding plaster. My hopes were soon realised as whole sections fell and crumbled to dust on the floor far below. Now I had excavated a small ledge above me and with a handhold my progress had no thought of time. My handhold had now become, not a ledge, but a step similar to those in the spiral staircase of the East Tower. Confirmation soon came with more bare handed digging which uncovered another step below the first, and the broken stairwell was now exposed.

Instead of wearying from this laborious task, I had grown more eager to pursue my discovery, and the evening hours flew by uncounted. A third step now emerged from the powdery dust but as well there now appeared directly behind it, a solid wall of stone barring further passage in that direction. I should have left then but I could no more down tools than stop breathing. Tapping on the walls of my new found staircase I searched for direction in the echo from my hammer and in minutes to my left, at shoulder height, the wall resonance changed.

I had not stopped to consider why the wall should be hollow at a level higher than the course of the stairwell, the mere fact that before me lay a cavity which had perhaps been exposed to no other eyes than mine in centuries spurred me on.

As the opening which I had created was now deep enough to require extra lighting, I decided to go back down to the courtyard to get the emergency lamp stored in the glove box of my car. Again I had the opportunity to stop and leave the Castle but I was compelled by a force greater than mere curiosity to continue and armed with my lamp to dispel the shadows I climbed the ladder, trained the light on the hollow wall and taking the chisel in my left hand I struck hard.

The sound which was heard then will never leave me, the metallic clang of hammered stone was only an echo to the shrill cry of a mortally wounded being. A shriek so piercing that my chisel quivered like a tuning fork and the walls trembled around me. In shock still, the cry then changed from hurt to an anguished wail and a low voice sorrowfully intoned one word, 'NO!'.

These sounds had exploded from the hole which I had pierced in the wall before me; the chisel having plunged in and out of sight leaving only a small round aperture.

Long moments passed, silence returned except for the thumping of my heart. I lay down my hammer, took up the lamp, and with a last look around I stepped out on to the beams above my waiting ladder. It struck me then that the air was no longer fragrant; it had in fact become heavy with the damp cellar smell of fungus and charged with an oppressive throbbing force. An atmosphere of growing hostility now hastened my departure, when suddenly I was struck full in the chest and thrown backwards by an invisible fist. No longer could I blame my imagination for my unease as I crawled out to the ladder and scarcely touching a single rung I hit the floor of the Great Hall and ran for the staircase. Another shrieking scream so loud it could be felt gave wings to my departure. In a flash I reached the landing and like flotsam in a whirlpool I plunged headlong down the stairs to burst out into the dark and silent courtyard.

The cool night air soon slowed my racing heart and gasping lungs. Some stars appeared and in their light, like mute sentries, the tall trees stood motionless.

A swarm of bats fluttering around the battlements indicated that it was time only for creatures of the night and I must leave.

Yet though my room at the nearby inn was never more attractive, I thought what foolishness; how stupid of me to be chased for my life by nothing more than my own senseless fear. A phantom sound which could have come from creaking boards or a bird trapped in the chimney, drove me in blind panic from my home and I resolved then that there would be no mystery here. In my flight I had of course dropped all of my tools including the flashlight, and the only lights in the Castle were those which I had strung up from the newly installed fusebox on the ground floor. So to switch them off I knew that I had to go back in, find the fuse box, and having switched off, make my way back to the door in total darkness. I knew that to hesitate would mean an end to my resolve so I started up the car, turned it to face the Castle door, and with the engine running I switched the headlights on full beam. This action I persuaded myself was not at all from fear but merely to prevent losing the door key. Thus inspired I reentered through the massive studded door, but with caution I ensured that it would remain wide open to permit, if need be, a hasty exit.

With a wedge used for just that purpose I pushed the door back to the wall, checked the lock to ensure that it would open with the turning of the handle, and made my way warily to the power source. Once there, I did not hesitate, pushed the lever and the place was plunged into total darkness. Catching my breath and my composure I groped my way like a blind man, step by step along the passageway back to the open door. There was no lightening of the gloom as I neared the front door; how could that be? had the lights failed in my car? No, the door was closed! icy fingers seemed to clutch me from behind pulling me deeper into the darkness and as my grip on the door knob tensed, I was suddenly imbued with inhuman strength and tore the lock out of the timbers and the door flew open. The reassuring hum of my car's running engine greeted me; and without hesitation I had it in gear and away, roaring at full throttle down the driveway to the open road and freedom.

Back in my hotel room, comfortable and safe in bed; I spent the remaining hours of darkness reading (another man's) account of strange happenings at Castle Stuart, with the gnawing fear that the final chapter of my own story was about to begin ...

THE MYSTERY OF CASTLE STUART

CHAPTER I

THE CASTLE

Castle Stuart, one of the oldest and most historic Castles in the north, is situated in the parish of Petty, some five miles due east from the town of Inverness. It was built during the time of the clans, and to a visitor it looks anything but picturesque.

It has no winding drives, nicely-laid lawns, or beautiful gardens; just a lone, solitary Castle, built in a large open field. It is said that from this ancient Castle the Earl of Moray takes his title. It is unoccupied. If you ask a native the reason, you will undoubtedly be told "It's haunted".

The Castle has a strange story connected with it, and, like a heritage, it has been handed down from father to son for many generations.

Many years ago the Earl of Moray of that time came to stay in the Castle. He had two reasons for doing so. His grandfather was a great sporting man, who lost heavily on horse racing and various other sports. When this young Earl came into the estate he found it heavily burdened with debt, which he wanted to clear off. He would save expenses by living in the Castle, not having the large parties, society dances, and other merry life which he found to be a heavy burden on his purse in the city of London. For another reason, it being a wide agricultural district, he intended to learn all the arts connected with farming, thus profiting by the way. The people were delighted to hear that the Earl was coming to stay among them as a farmer. On his arrival with his large staff of servants, the tenantry turned out to give him a real Highland welcome. Bonfires were lit, toasts were pledged, wishing long life and success to the Earl. A week after his arrival he suddenly left with his whole staff for the south. He told no one the reason, and many wondered. It was thought business matters concerning the estate took him away, and everyone expected him shortly to return. Weeks passed, but no word of the Earl. Then some of the gossips got something to talk about, when an officer came to stay there. He was a major in an English foot regiment, then stationed at Fort

George, and was newly home after serving in foreign parts, where he won great honours, his breast being covered with medals and decorations for his bravery in the battlefields. He took the Castle for a period of six months, but did not stay that time. A week only elapsed and then he left. It was rumoured he had a nervous breakdown owing to his long service abroad and was recuperating his health somewhere in the south of England. But he never returned, and during the remainder of the six months the Castle stood empty. The next tenant was a gentleman from London, who was reputed to be immensely wealthy. He intended to write a book on historical places in the Highlands, but unfortunately did not remain long enough to do so. In less than a week he also left for the south, otherwise he might have found plenty of historical work in writing a book about the Castle. So the place was again empty, and strange stories got around about it being haunted. The natives would not venture near it, nor pass by it after dark, and many a strange tale was told about it as they sat round their peat fires on a winter's evening.

For a year the Castle remained empty.

CHAPTER II

THE EARL AND HIS FACTOR

One day the Earl of Moray and his factor were discussing estate matters, when the Factor brought the Castle into the subject of conversation.

"We must get the place let to someone. It is really a white elephant as it stands," he said.

"And will probably remain so," answered the Earl, "the Castle is haunted."

"Nonsense," said the Factor, "nothing but simpleminded and superstitious people with their foolish stories, making mountains out of molehills. If I could only find who invented these stories I would give them a bigger fright than what's haunting the Castle."

"Indeed," said the Earl, "so you don't believe it is haunted?"

"No, sir, certainly not," said the Factor, "there is nothing unnatural about the place to frighten anyone."

"I am glad to hear that," said the Earl, "but how do you account for myself and the other gentlemen leaving it so suddenly?"

"As regards yourself, sir," replied the Factor, "I never thought it would be a suitable place for you to stay in. You are a young man, and youth craves for enjoyment. There is no society for you to mix with here, or other amusements which you have been accustomed to . It is far too lonely a place for such a young man."

"You have made a mistake with your thoughts," said the Earl, "I was forced to leave it."

"Did you meet the ghost then?" queried the Factor.

"Not exactly," remarked the Earl, "but my servants saw some strange sights."

"Indeed!" said the Factor, in a surprised tone.

"Yes," said the Earl, "it was my valet and my butler who first drew my attention to it. My room was on the ground floor, while they slept in an upstairs room. A night or two after our arrival those men who slept in

3

the same room heard heavy footsteps ascending the stairs about midnight, and they wondered very much who it could be. Shortly after they heard a terrible noise, followed by loud screams, which seemed to come from a room further up the stair. They were terribly frightened, but passed no remarks next day. The following night they determined to keep watch, and, sure enough, about the moment of twelve, they again heard the footsteps. The stairway wound up past their room, and when they heard the footsteps sounding near enough they opened the door, and, flashing a light on the intruder, they got the shock of their lives when they saw the form of a headless Highlander ascending the stair. Quickly they closed the door till the footsteps passed, then both came rushing down and bounded into my room in a very excited state to inform me of what they had seen. I dressed, and immediately went up to their room. There I heard a dreadful noise in the room above, and was on the point of going up to investigate when I heard a most unearthly scream that made my blood turn cold. Next day I left the Castle."

"They got the shock of their lives when they saw the headless Highlander ascending the stair."

"Dear me, that is a strange story," said the Factor. "Is there no accounting for it?"

"Perhaps there is," said the Earl, "if I knew something more regarding the history of the Castle. I suppose, being such a long time on the estate, you know something of its history?"

Some time later the Earl was seated in an easy chair beside the fire in the Factor's office, smoking a cigar. He was a tall, handsome, young man, with fresh complexion, fair hair and sparkling blue eyes. He was about twenty-six years of age, and had only come into the Earldom a year or so previously on the death of his father. Like his grandfather, he was a great sportsman – fond of horses, a good rider, and a splendid shot. A pleasant young man also, he was fond of a joke, possessed no pride of rank, and was extremely kind to his tenantry and cottars. In society circles he was largely sought after, and it was whispered that more than one worthy lady had an eye on him with a view to matrimony.

As to the Factor, he was an old, stern-looking man, who had served over fifty years with the young Earl's father and grandfather. He was, moreover, a severe man, and hated by the tenantry for his harsh methods. His father had been a lawyer, whose fame was known far and near, for his great abilities. When a young man, the Factor entered the banking profession, but after several years he left the bank, joined his father, and also became an excellent lawyer. When his father died, he became factor and lawyer for the Moray estate.

"History," grunted the Factor, removing his glasses, and looking round towards the Earl from his desk, where he was examining some documents, "you want to hear the history of the Castle? Well, it came into your family possessions in the reign of James V. This part of your property, or estate, begins at the village of Campbelltown, and extends along the coast for six or seven miles, until you join Forbes of Culloden's estate, near Inverness. In breadth it varies from a mile to perhaps three at its widest part. This district is called Petty, or Stuarton. It is an agricultural district, with very rich soil, and has several large farms on it. The people in Campbelltown, and those nearest the sea at Petty, have successful fishings in that part of the Moray Firth. They follow the calling of fishermen, have several good boats and reap a rich harvest from the sea. It was during the days of the clan risings that your forefathers had grave fears of losing this part of the estate. The clans were a wild, thieving gang of ruffians, always on the warpath, fighting with each other, or like a horde of desert

5

Bedouins, ready to cut one another's throats for plunder. So long as these clans fought among themselves it was perfectly safe, but when they were at peace with each other then others had to look out. They came like a pack of wolves in search of prey. I will give you an illustration. The chief of the Clan Fraser had a pretty daughter, and the McIntosh Chief fancied her for a wife. McIntosh knew if he went to ask her hand in marriage he would be refused by her father, if not by herself. So McIntosh gathered his clan, attacked the Frasers by surprise and defeated them, and carried the daughter away by force. The Fraser chief sent a messenger to the Chief of Clan Cameron inviting him to a big supper. During the feast he told how the McIntoshes had stolen his daughter. So that night they invented plans and vowed vengeance over rusty swords and decanters of whisky how they would make the McIntosh clan reek in blood. On a certain night both clans were to attack the McIntoshes. Cameron had his clan ambushed in a different part from where the Frasers were to make their attack, and McIntosh, thinking Fraser had come for revenge, engaged him in combat. The Frasers kept retiring, thus drawing the McIntoshes from their stronghold. As soon as they got them far enough away from their positions the Camerons rushed in from behind and a fierce fight ensued. The McIntoshes were defeated and Fraser got his daughter back. But that did not satisfy the Camerons. They gathered all the horses, cattle, sheep and goats they could lay hands on belonging to the McIntoshes and then took their departure. There was peace among them for a while after that, but it did not keep them from raids on other people's property who had no clan or armed party to fight for them. At length an attack was made on Castle Stuart. I should not say attack, for the Earl who owned the estate at that time made no attempt to defend the Castle, he simply removed all the valuables and left them the building. It angered them when the Earl refused to give fight. In that way the Castle changed owners nearly a dozen times, one clan driving out the other. They did not leave, however, without stealing nearly all the horses, cattle and sheep in the district. The farmers were in an awful dilemma and went to the Earl seeking protection. What could the Earl do? He had no clan and could not protect himself. He tried to make up their losses but it cost him a lot of money and would probably have ruined him if it had not been for Culloden. Cumberland stopped the clans' devilment. He scattered and chased them to their glens, which they never left again. And thus, after a number of years, the Castle was restored once again to its rightful owners."

"Strange history indeed," said the Earl, "no wonder it is full of ghosts."

"I can hardly credit these stories," said the Factor, "but if you think it haunted, sir, have you any idea of a plan to get the mystery solved?"

"Yes, I was thinking of a plan," remarked the Earl carelessly.

The Factor, who had been standing with his back against the desk while relating the history of the Castle, adjusted his glasses and, in his stern manner, asked the Earl about the plan he had in view.

"I have already referred to a certain room in the Castle being haunted," said the Earl. "I suggest we both go and stay in that room for a night. We can take turn about at keeping watch, and I am certain we shall find out something."

The Factor turned a ghastly colour, and clutched the table for support. For several minutes he could not speak. When he did find his voice he stammered, "Yes, we will find something. We will find death!"

The Earl was looking at the fire, but at the Factor's strange remarks he turned sharply, and observed his almost fainting condition.

"Do you feel ill?" asked the Earl.

"Ill," replied the Factor, "you make me feel ill. You are surely mad! Stay in a haunted room for a night! It is ridiculous."

"I am sorry my suggestion unnerved you," said the Earl.

"Your suggestion is horrible," replied the Factor. "Imagine staying in a haunted room. It is past my comprehension. The thought of it would kill me. It may please a young man seeking adventure, but I am not fit for that sort of work, and was never asked to do such a thing. For upwards of fifty years I have served both your beloved father and grandfather. I served them honestly and faithfully, and many a bizarre transaction I have carried through for them. I was relentless in my work – jailed men for debt, drove many from their homes without mercy, and it was said of me that I put many to an early grave; but in all my experience I was never asked to undertake such a task as you suggest – to watch for ghosts! No!

7

Whatever suffering I may have caused the living, I will have no dealings with the dead."

"Perhaps it would not be very pleasant," said the Earl. "It is no good thinking of letting the Castle until we get the mystery cleared up."

"Humph," grunted the Factor, "I don't think ghost – hunting comes under my category as your estate agent."

"Perhaps not," remarked the Earl. "I will go myself and stay for a night."

The Earl then rose from his seat, and was pulling on his gloves, when the Factor, who was putting certain papers in his desk, turned towards him and said, "I don't think it is advisable, sir. There is an instance that has come to my memory; it happened over thirty years ago. There was a certain farmer who had a house on the estate for his ploughmen. It was a splendid house, but no ploughman would remain any length of time with him. They all complained of the house being haunted. At length no ploughman would engage with him, and he came to me raging in an awful temper. I advised him to get someone to watch and find out the trouble. He was very angry with me, but I told him I was not paid for watching haunted houses. So he went away. Some time later someone advised him to go and explain his case to the minister, which he did, and the minister undertook to go and keep watch. He arrived one evening at the house and stayed in one of the rooms which was prepared for him. At twelve o'clock he heard the front door being opened, and then the door of the room in which he was sitting also opened. He then saw the ghastly form of a skeleton appear in the doorway. He boldly demanded to know what it wanted by disturbing that house. The ghost, in a sepulchral tone, made reply, "I was a mason to trade and at the building of this house was murdered by my companions and my body buried under the stone at the front door. If you will have my bones removed, and buried with my kindred in the churchyard of Petty, I will be at rest.' This was done, and there never was a ghostly sound heard in that house after."

"That is a remarkable story," said the Earl, "and makes my flesh creep. I would never attempt to solve the Castle Stuart mystery if I thought of meeting a spectre of that kind."

"Ah! you are becoming a little more sensible now," said the Factor, "youth thirsts for adventure but sometimes gets more than its fill. Take my advice, and consult the minister; he will undoubtedly help you, perhaps have some theory of investigation."

"You will write the minister, then," said the Earl, "give him my compliments, and inform him of my intended early visit."

When the Earl took his departure, the Factor seated himself beside the fire to think over matters. "Humph," he grunted, "the Earl is like a mad horse. If I did not keep a tight rein on him we would be over the precipice. He will require a lot of breaking in to tame him. To think I would go and watch for ghosts in a haunted room! It is absurd. What are factors coming to? I plainly see my days are numbered. It will require a younger man to keep up the pace as things are moving at present. But I must get that letter to the minister done."

"He then saw the ghastly form of a skeleton appear in the doorway."

CHAPTER III

THE MINISTER

The minister of the district at that time was a tall, athletic young man of about thirty years of age. He had only been a year previously ordained in the parish, the previous minister having passed away. This young man was an eminent scholar and a powerful preacher. In his college days he was reputed to be an excellent boxer, and few could beat him at feats of strength. Of a cheery disposition, he was beloved by the people for his interest in their welfare and his kindly actions to the poor. He received the Factor's letter, informing him of the intended visit from the Earl, and a day or so later the Earl and his factor arrived. The minister gave them a warm welcome, and led them into his study. After they were comfortably seated, the Factor opened the subject of the Castle and told him its strange history, while the Minister listened attentively.

"Do you believe in ghosts haunting a place?" said the Earl, turning towards the minister, who was sitting on a chair beside them, round the fire.

"I am not a disbeliever in anything," said the minister. "If you read the thirty-second chapter of Genesis, verse twenty-four, you will find there how Jacob wrestled with a spirit. I never met a ghost, although I have seen some strange things on my travels late and early, among the sick and dying. I have several times met that strange blue light which is said to be the forerunner of a death. On one occasion, when returning home very late, I met a phantom funeral. I also knew who's funeral it was, and a day or so later the woman died. Further than what I have told you, I have met nothing unnatural. The only remedy, if a place is haunted, is to watch and find out what is haunting it."

"It is a ghastly proposition, watching for ghosts in a lonely, haunted Castle," said the Factor, "only a raving madman would undertake such a task."

"The fishing depends on the bait you use," returned the minister. "The proverb says 'money is the root of all evil'. You will get people to face the devil for money, let alone a ghost."

"You mean we should offer a reward in money," queried the Earl. "Sounds a splendid idea. How much would you suggest giving?"

"Get the man before you make suggestions," said the Factor, looking over his glasses at the minister.

The minister lit his pipe. He was seriously thinking. "You have come to consult me, gentlemen," he said "to get my candid opinion about the Castle. Perhaps you expect me to solve the mystery. I might, or I might not. Let me explain some peculiar characteristics in people. There are some born of a very nervous, imaginary disposition, who really believe they see unearthly things. There are others born with the gift of second-sight. They are generally meeting phantom funerals, or seeing strange sights. If such people were put into a haunted place, one could hardly credit their story. As regards Castle Stuart, suppose we get four men – I shall offer myself as one of them – and each be locked in the haunted room for a night. Whatever is heard or seen in the room during the night must be kept secret until each has had his turn. The following night we shall all meet here and each will tell his own story. I am almost certain some of us will be able to give an account of the mystery."

"That is an excellent plan," said the Earl, "but how much of a reward am I to offer?" he asked.

The factor rose, and walked leisurely across the room, deep in thought. At length, turning to the Earl, he said, "It is a very unpleasant task this, and full of grave danger. The suspense of waiting in that lonely room is enough to wreck the strongest nerve, but if they should solve the mystery it will repay us. I should think £20 for each man a very reasonable sum."

The Earl willingly agreed, and it was left to the minister to find the men. He was also to inform the Earl when everything was in readiness, as he wished to meet the men personally before they undertook the task.

CHAPTER IV

ROB ANGUS

The minister went about his task without loss of time. He caused notices to be put up, asking for three volunteers, also stating the reward, and setting forth what each had to do. A night or two later, while the minister was busy in his study, a massive giant of a man entered the room.

"Well, my good man, do you wish to see me," said the minister, as he shook the giant's hand and motioned him to a chair.

"I have come to see you, minister," blustered out the man, "about that ploy up at the Castle. I was reading your notice wanting three men. If you have not already got them, put me on your list. My name is Rob Angus."

"Bravo! you are my first applicant," said the minister, smiling. "Do you work in this district?"

The big man gave a loud laugh, and then replied, "It depends on what you call work. I do a bit at poaching and mole-catching in my spare time, when I am not engaged at my regular trade."

"What trade do you generally follow?" inquired the minister.

"Now you are asking questions that cannot well be answered," said Rob. "There is more than you anxious to know that - Rob Fraser, the gauger for one. I am a man of many parts: I can turn my hand to several jobs."

"Are you not afraid of the poaching trade?" asked the minister.

"Afraid of what!" roared Rob.

"Of being caught by the gamekeepers," said the minister. "It is a pretty stiff sentence you will get, I am told, for poaching."

Rob gave a loud laugh. "I am afraid of no living man, reptile, bird or beast," said he, "but I will tell you a good story about gamekeepers. Some time ago I heard that the Earl's party were coming to shoot on the low grounds. I did not grudge the Earl's party what they killed. It was the birds they frightened to death that I grudged. If I did not get there first, these birds would be miles away. So I took my gun and my dog and made for the fields, where I knew I could get a good bag of mixed game. I had a splendid shooting - three bundles; as much as I could carry on my shoulders; all kinds of game. I was making my way home in the evening, with one of my loads, when who should appear from behind some bushes but three gamekeepers, dressed in their fancy grey knickerbocker suits. 'Hold on, there,' they shouted. 'Hand over that game and look damn quick about it.' They were about a hundred yards away from me at the time. 'All right gentlemen,' I said, using my best civility and walking towards them, but when they saw me coming they took to their heels. So, just to test their speed, I fired a shot after them, but they were well out of range. Believe me, sir, they would not have disgraced a sprinter. Some time later I got a letter from the factor, threatening to evict me from my wee bit hoose. It is not much of a hoose, minister, but my father built it himself. It has but clay walls and is roofed with heather; still it suits me all right. I went down to the factor's office next day and walked boldly in. He was looking at some documents in an old desk, the dirty skinflint, and glowered at me like an owl through his glasses. I never spoke a word but went over and caught him by the throat, and gave it a bit of a squeeze. He turned black as night in the face, and his tongue came out of his mouth, nearly a foot long! 'Look here,' I said, 'if ever you dare threaten me again, I will make more than my rent out of your dirty old carcass by taking it along to Dr Crombie - the doctor's daft for dead bodies!' And from that day to this the factor or his keepers never troubled me. But I

"He turned black as night in the face, and his tongue came out of his mouth, nearly a foot long!"

must be going, sir," he concluded, rising. "When you require me you will have no trouble in finding Rob Angus."

The minister was highly amused at the big man's story, and for a long while after he left he could not help wondering at his fearful size, enormous strength, and reckless daring.

CHAPTER V

THE ELDER

At the time of which this story treats, the poor uneducated people lived in fear of such men as earls, factors and ministers. The Earls of Moray the good folks of Petty seldom saw, but both the factor and the minister held them well in esteem.

They were looked upon as very important persons, and the humble, hard-working peasants hoped to find favour in their sight by keeping their laws and obeying their commands.

Several days had elapsed since the events narrated in the foregoing chapter had occurred but no further volunteers came to offer their services to the minister. One night, however, there was a meeting of the Kirk Session and, at the close of the meeting, the minister invited the ruling elder into his study. Having talked for a while on church matters, the minister finally brought Castle Stuart into the conversation. He explained to the elder all about the Earl's visit, the plan he intended to execute, and the splendid reward he was offering for a solution to the mystery of the so-called haunted castle.

"Do you know Rob Angus?" asked the minister.

"Rob Angus!" shouted the elder. "Who does not know him? He is a bad man, Rob, with his poaching, smuggling, and drinking. Are you acquainted with him, sir?"

"I only met him once," said the minister. "He came to the manse the other night to offer his services to unravel the castle mystery. Such a powerful man, I could not help but admire him."

"There is nothing to admire about him," said the elder, "unless it is his sinful ways."

"He is a brave man," said the minister.

"There is no doubt about that," answered the elder; "he would take a lamb out of a lion's mouth! He nearly shot the Earl's gamekeepers and almost strangled the life out of the factor, who was a week in bed over it."

"I admire him as a brave man, for all his faults," said the minister. "He is the only man that has so far come forward to offer his services. I am rather disappointed no others have come to my assistance after the splendid reward offered by the Earl. I am certain he will be very angry about it. I would deem it a great favour if you would consent to come as one of the party."

"Me!" shouted the elder, "surely there are plenty younger men to be got without dragging in an old man like me to go watching in a haunted castle."

"The young men I expected have failed me," said the minister, "that is why I ask you."

"Perhaps yourself and Angus will be sufficient," suggested the elder. "Is it necessary to have so many?"

"I promised to get four men," said the minister, "but I am thinking, myself and my brave friend, Angus, will have to undertake the task ourselves."

"Ach! I am sick of hearing that man's name mentioned," said the elder.

These remarks, uttered in such a sarcastic manner, angered the minister. He looked savagely at the elder, and said "that is quite enough. I don't want to hear any more of that. Rob Angus is the only Christian in the district. He laughs to scorn what God-fearing men like you are afraid of. It is ill on your part to remark so harshly about him. When your wife was sick, about a year ago, you got a couple of rabbits, a wild duck, or a pheasant every morning on your doorstep. Who put them there? That dirty man, Rob Angus!"

"I never heard of that before," stammered the elder, "I thought it was the keeper."

"Did you ever ask the keeper?" said the minister. "It was your neighbours who told me. You will remember when Widow Scott's child took suddenly ill one night, how she ran knocking at all her neighbours' doors, and they never let on they heard her. But big Rob Angus heard her knocks, and rose and went for the doctor, aye, and that, too, in a raging blizzard. Every morning while the child lay ill he brought a couple of fresh rabbits, and he went to the town for medicine, when it could not be got elsewhere – fourteen miles altogether, through wreaths of snow up to his waist. Widow Scott told me the story herself, with tears streaming down her cheeks. That is Rob Angus, the big, quiet, silent man!"

"I am sorry, sir, that I spoke so nasty about him," said the elder. "He is a good neighbour, and never interferes with other people's business. If only he would give over his wicked ways."

"Let his wicked ways alone," said the minister, "that is my work. I only wish there were more like him in the parish. When I inform the Earl, Angus will be placed very high in his estimation."

There was always jealousy when a poor man became a personal favourite with the Earl, so it did not please the elder to hear of Rob Angus being placed in such a position.

"If I should be doing a favour to the Earl by going to the Castle," said the elder, "I am ready and willing to help both of you."

"Thank you," said the minister. "As an elder of my church, and a God-fearing man, you have assisted me in many matters, and there is nothing to fear in helping me now. No evil can harm a godly man, who walketh in the strength of the Lord. He tells you, 'be not afraid, for I am with thee,' or, as the psalmist says, 'although I walk through death's dark vale yet I will fear no ill.'"

After bidding the minister good-night, the elder took his departure. On his homeward journey he had many things to think over. This was a different minister from the last one. There were none fallen so low but he would lift up, and set their feet upon a rock. He was the good shepherd in thought, word and deed.

When the elder arrived home his wife was waiting for him.

"You are late the night," she said, "surely the kirk session meeting was finished before now?"

"Yes," said the elder, "but I was in the manse with the minister."

"And what was he speaking about?" she asked, as she poured him out a cup of coffee.

"About church matters, and inquiring about Rob Angus. Rob was at the manse and he is going to watch at the Castle," replied the elder.

"A good man for the job," said his wife, "there is not a ghost in the Castle will frighten Rob."

17

"Do you remember the rabbits and pheasants we used to get at the door when you were sick?" asked the elder.

"Yes," replied his wife, "what about them?"

"Did you ever hear who put them there?" asked the elder.

"Yes," said his wife carelessly, "Rob Angus did. Who other would put them there?"

"You never told me that," said the elder.

"I thought you knew," answered his wife, "but why are you asking?"

"Because the minister made remarks about it tonight," said the elder.

"How did the minister happen to speak about that?" asked his wife.

"Ach! I don't know," grunted the elder.

"Who is going besides Rob and the minister?" asked his wife.

"I am," said the elder.

"What? you are surely daft," shouted his wife.

"Daft or not daft, the minister specially requires me there," said the elder. "If I am a pillar of the temple I must support it."

"What has the Castle to do with the temple?" demanded his wife angrily. "Did you promise the minister you would go?"

"Yes, certainly, I promised," said the elder.

"You are not to go then," said his wife, "I will see the minister myself about it. He has a good impudence to ask you. And you should not have promised. You have often heard my old father relate about what is haunting that dirty old Castle."

"Ach! I am not in a mood to hear about that story just now," returned the elder. "I promised to go, and I am going; that is all about it."

CHAPTER VI
THE SHOEMAKER

The day after the meeting of the kirk session the minister was visiting several of his flock, and on his homeward journey he made a call on McDougall, the shoemaker. At one end of his house was the shop where the shoemaker worked, and the village worthies generally gathered there to discuss important events or happenings in the district. The old man, in this way, had always the latest information. When the minister called, the shoemaker was alone, busily engaged mending a pair of shoes. After a friendly greeting, the minister seated himself on the bench for a chat. The shoemaker was a noted singer, and for nearly thirty years had acted as precentor in the church. He had also had a large and well-trained choir, but had retired from the precentorship a year before the minister came to the district, but he was still interested in singing and the welfare of the church. He related to the minister many stories of different choirs he had conducted and the abilities of several singers he had trained. The minister sat intently watching the shoemaker stitching a piece of sole leather on to the shoe. The shop overlooked the main road, and who should happen to pass but a gamekeeper, dressed in a fine grey suit, a gun under his arm, and a spaniel dog at his heels. The minister happened to observe him pass, and remarked– "That man seems to have a very pleasant job."

"It is pleasant enough just now," said the shoemaker, bursting into a fit of laughter, "but it is not so pleasant when big Rob Angus is about."

"Indeed," said the minister, joining in the shoemaker's mirth, "they are afraid of Angus then?"

"They are all terrified of him," said the shoemaker, "factors, gaugers, and all. Rob is a laird all on his own. I am hearing he has volunteered to lure the ghost in the Castle."

"He has that," said the minister.

The shoemaker wanted to know who were all going, and was determined he would get the minister to tell him, for he dearly loved gossip, and was moreover a bit of a boaster. "You would have got plenty volunteers?" queried the shoemaker, busily stitching.

19

"Oh yes," answered the minister carelessly.

"I think the young Earl must be daft, throwing away so much money," said the shoemaker. "There is nothing to be frightened of in the Castle. It is nothing but old wives tales about it being haunted."

"Indeed," retorted the minister.

"There were some chaps here the other night," went on the shoemaker, "and it was a real treat to listen to their stories of the different kinds of ghosts they said haunted the Castle. I told them it would be the easiest made money that ever was earned in this parish. A perfect gold mine."

"You do not think the Castle is haunted?" asked the minister.

"Not a bit of it," replied the shoemaker.

"Who is going besides yourself and Angus?"

"Your neighbour, the elder, and yourself, souter!"

"Me!" exclaimed the shoemaker, rising and dropping the shoe, "I was never asked to go."

"You are asked now," said the minister. "I only required one more man for my party, and it is as well for you to get the £20 as any other. It is easy earned money, especially when the Castle is, as you say, not haunted. I will write the Earl tonight, and inform him that I have my men ready. He wishes to meet you all personally at the manse tomorrow evening. I will let you know the hour later."

Thanking the shoemaker, and bidding him good evening, the minister took his departure, leaving the shoemaker in a terrible dilemma. Locking the shop door he went through to the kitchen.

"What is the matter with you?" asked his wife, looking anxiously at him.

"I am in a fearful predicament," said the shoemaker, throwing himself on a chair.

"Calm yourself and do not be so excited," said his wife.

"It is easy for you to speak like that," said the shoemaker, "but if you were in my position you would whistle another tune."

The shoemaker then told his wife all about the minister's visit and how he had been trapped into going to the Castle.

His wife stood looking at him stupidly while he related his story, and then said – "It serves you right, I knew that gabbing tongue of yours would get you into trouble some day. What did you say to him?"

"He gave me no chance to say anything," answered the shoemaker. "I believe he just came on purpose to get me."

"Well, well," said his wife, "he has got a poor specimen of a man in you to go hunting for ghosts."

On his homeward journey the minister felt highly delighted at how neatly he had trapped the shoemaker. He had only walked about a mile when he met Rob Angus with a gun under his arm and two wild ducks slung across his back.

"Good evening, Angus," said the minister, "I took you for a gamekeeper."

"God forbid that anyone should mistake me for one of them, sir" returned Angus, "but here is a present of a grand pair of ducks for your dinner, if you are not too proud to take them."

"Thank you, Angus," said the minister, taking the proffered gift.

"I hope you will not thank the keepers for them, like the party I once knew," said Angus.

"Let me hear that story," said the minister.

"Well, some time ago there was a poor family in this district," began Angus, "and I used to throw a rabbit or a hare on their doorstep occasionally. They thought it was the keeper that sent the kind gifts, so one day the good-wife thanked him."

'Och, that was nothing,' said the keeper plausibly, 'I always like being kind to the poor.' A day or so later that same keeper caught her husband setting a snare and had him brought to court for it. He got twenty days from the Sheriff. That was the keeper's way of helping the poor. I trust the woman still values his kindness. But I got level with that keeper today. I watched him last night setting snares round a turnip field below the village. He had about eighty snares set, and I took a turn round this morning about four o'clock and got over forty rabbits.

He will not have a big bag this morning. But it is the early bird that catches the worm! He will have to rise early to beat Rob Angus."

"When he finds that rabbits have been taken out of his snares," said the minister, "will he not make a row?"

"It is little I care for what he finds, or what row he makes," said Rob. "I swore I would get my revenge on a wolf like him, pretending to poor people to be a good Samaritan."

The minister smiled at the big man's remarks, and said, "I have got all my volunteers now for the Castle business."

"Oh! I heard you got the elder," said Angus.

"Well, I am just after getting the shoemaker, too," said the minister, and he laughingly told Angus the story.

Rob burst into a fit of laughter. "I would rather than twenty pounds to be near the shoemaker when they lock him in the haunted room," he said, "the poor man will go crazy."

"The Earl wants to meet you all at the manse tomorrow evening," said the minister, "and I trust you will be able to come, as the necessary arrangements are to be made."

Angus, having given the minister his promise to be present, each took their different ways.

"Here is a present of a grand pair of ducks for your dinner."

22

CHAPTER VII

MEETING THE EARL

The Earl arrived at the manse the following night, and was told the whole story by the minister of how he got his men, and his Lordship laughed heartily over how the shoemaker had been caught. Shortly after, the elder and the shoemaker arrived together, and were introduced to the Earl, who shook hands with them, then motioned them to a chair by the fire. Both looked worried and very downhearted, so the Earl, in an endeavour to cheer them up, related some humorous stories, while the minister delighted the Earl by telling several amusing exploits about Rob Angus. At last Rob arrived.

The Earl, having heard so much about the big man, was anxious to meet him. He rose and cordially shook hands with him, remarking, "I am pleased to meet you, Angus."

"That is more than some of your employees would be," said Angus, and the Earl laughed at Rob's sally.

After all had got seated the Earl started quizzing Rob on his career, and at length asked him if he had ever met anything that frightened him.

"Well," remarked Rob thoughtfully, " I have wandered about at all hours of the night and morning and have been in some strange places in my time, but it was only once I got a bit scared."

"Let us hear the story," said the Earl, settling back comfortably in an easy chair.

"It happened several years ago," said Rob. "I was working at the harvest on Castle Stuart Farm, and when I was finished I got paid off. I went the following day to Inverness, where I met several old acquaintances in a public house, and what between drams and stories about old times the hours flew past till closing time, when I took the road for home. It was a fine, clear moonlit night, and I set off intending to take the road along the seashore, after passing the marsh, to see if any wild ducks were about. However, when I arrived at the marsh I was surprised to observe a man leaning against a fence at the side of the road. As I passed I remarked that it was a fine night. 'Not bad,' he answered, 'are you going far?' 'To Petty,' I replied. 'Same direction as myself,' he said, 'do

23

you object to my company?' 'I object to no social company,' I said. 'Right,' he answered, and swung into the same stride as myself. 'Are you acquaint in this part of the country?' I asked my companion. 'Oh, I know a few here,' he replied. As we stepped along I had a good look at him. He was a tall, slightly-built man with sharp features, dark complexion, long Roman nose and dark piercing eyes. He was well dressed and carried a cane. We walked along for a bit in silence, then he suddenly stopped, pulled a bottle from his pocket and handed it to me, saying, 'Have a drink!' I took a good swig from the bottle; it was the finest blend whisky I ever put over my throat – and I reckon myself a fair judge. 'Some whisky, that,' I remarked. He smiled, but did not taste himself, and put the bottle back into his pocket. He seemed to know every place we passed and everybody in the parish. 'You are no stranger in these parts?' I remarked. He smiled but did not speak till after we had passed Allenfearn, when he pointed with his cane and said 'That's Balloch up there.' 'Yes,' I affirmed, 'that's Balloch village; are you acquaint there?' 'I know a few of the folks,' he answered. He apparently knew everyone, but would answer no questions although he kept asking plenty. Further along we rested at the roadside, and I had another drink out of his bottle. We were newsing away, and I began to fill my pipe for a smoke. In doing so the lid fell to the ground and I was bending down looking for it when I got the biggest shock of my life. Instead of feet, my companion had cloven hooves! I really believe if it had not been for the amount of whisky I had consumed I would have dropped dead with the shock. Gathering my senses together with an effort I remarked in a quavering voice, 'We will better be moving.' With that he lit a cigar, and we proceeded on our way. He was a cheery enough companion and we jogged cannily along till we came to the entrance to Castle Stuart. 'This is my destination,' he then announced, 'I have some business up there,' and he pointed with his cane to the old castle. So I bade him good-night and proceeded on my homeward way. And that is the only unnatural thing I ever saw in my life."

"You are a brave man, Angus," said the Earl, "what a nerve you have got."

The elder and the shoemaker were sitting listening terrified at Rob's story. Their faces betrayed their nervous condition, for they both were white as death.

24

"I wish I had never heard that story," said the shoemaker "for I have been told it was the Evil One himself who haunts the Castle."

Ha, ha, ha, laughed Rob, till the tears were running down his cheeks.

"It is not a laughing matter," said the elder, "especially for us, but you and Satan are old friends."

To that Rob made no answer, but continued laughing so heartily that both the Earl and the minister were forced to join him.

At length the Earl, rising to depart, said, "By going to the Castle, you gentlemen are doing me a great favour, and so besides the twenty pounds I am offering as a reward I am also going to give each of you and your wives a life-rent of your houses. I shall always take an interest in your welfare, and I earnestly trust no harm will befall you in your brave attempt to solve the mystery of Castle Stuart."

It was agreed then that the minister stay the following night in the Castle, followed the next night by the elder then the shoemaker, and lastly by Angus, owing to him being busy at the smuggling trade, a boat having just arrived to take on board a cargo of whisky. It was further agreed that the bold adventurers arrive at the Castle by ten o'clock, and that the ground officer of the estate be waiting to show them to the haunted room.

CHAPTER VIII

SOLVING THE MYSTERY

On the following night the minister arrived at the Castle. It was a beautiful night towards the end of harvest, and a full moon shone in a cloudless sky. The ground officer, with a lantern in his hand, met him at the entrance gate.

"Good evening," greeted the minister, "have you been waiting long?"

"I have but newly arrived, sir," said the officer, and with that led the minister up the flight of stairs.

"This is the room, sir," he said, opening a door. The minister entered, and, after bidding him good-night, the officer locked the door and took his departure. It proved to be a large, airy room near the top of the Castle. A cheery peat fire threw a radiant heat from a large open hearth, on each side of which was placed a comfortable easy chair. In the centre of the room was a large mahogany table, on which stood a beautiful brass lamp, which fully illuminated the place, and ancient, heavy gilt-framed oil paintings by famous masters adorned the walls. Over the fireplace hung a magnificent mirror, which was tilted slightly forward, and reflected most of the furniture in the room, and an old-fashioned and neatly carved bookcase full of many valuable books stood in a corner.

"His slumber was, however, disturbed by a horrible dream."

26

The minister, after having a look around, lit his pipe, and, selecting a book, seated himself in one of the easy chairs to await events. Feeling very comfortable, and finding little interest in the story, he speedily fell fast asleep. His slumber was, however, disturbed by a horrible dream. At midnight he dreamt he heard the door being gently opened, and he saw what he took to be a big, sturdy Highlander, dressed in faded tartan, and armed with a dirk and claymore, enter. He came boldly forward and sat himself down in the easy chair on the opposite side of the hearth from the minister. He had a most gruesome appearance; his long, red, matted hair hung down over his shoulders, while a red bristling beard almost covered his face, the splatches of blood thereon in no way improving his countenance. For a while the stranger and the minister sat looking at each other in silence, then the Highlander, leaning forward, placed a large, bony hand on the minister's knee and, speaking in a deep, hollow tone of voice, said, "Did you come here on purpose to frighten me?" At the sound of a voice the minister awoke with a start. The fire was nearly out, so he stirred it up, put on more peats, and, looking at his watch, was astonished to discover that it was two o'clock in the morning. Going over to the window he drew aside the shutter and looked out. How beautiful it was. The moon shone clear as day and everything was calm and peaceful. For a while he thus stood, then, lighting his pipe, he went back to his chair and took up his book. He was just finishing the story when the officer came in the morning to unlock the door. So the minister's watch passed without much adventure.

The next night it was the elder's turn for duty. It seemed a weary day to him as he thought upon many old ghostly stories he had heard about the Castle. He was feeling as if it might be his last day on earth. That night he bade his wife good-bye, with a quiver on his lip, and with a trembling heart he set out for the Castle. The estate officer met him, as he had done the minister, and showed him to the room. He heard the door being locked and the footsteps of the man descending the stairs, then all was silent as the grave. In his nervousness, he imagined eerie sounds in the wind amongst the trees round the Castle, and got a terrible fright by the hooting of an owl. It sounded to him like some demon crying vengeance on such as he for trying to solve the mystery of things unearthly.

So he prayed aloud, and implored the Lord to protect him in that awesome place; to save him as he did Daniel in the lions' den; and to be his refuge and his strength, and not forsake him in the hour of trouble. Then, seating himself in one of the easy chairs, he began reading passages from his Bible. He was thus engaged when the door opened, and the same wild, fierce looking Highlander who had visited the minister made his appearance. He was armed with a dagger and a large sword hung by his side. The elder had intended to ask whenever he saw it, "What seeketh thou?" but words failed him, he was so stunned by the awful apparition which now confronted him. He felt cold all over, then broke into a sweat, which ran in big drops over his face, nearly blinding him. He felt paralysed in every limb, his whole strength seeming to have left him. Stepping forward, the newcomer took a seat in the chair opposite the poor elder, who could do nothing but gaze in fear at the ghastly figure. While he was thus gazing, he happened to observe a movement in the mirror, and, looking up, saw reflected therein the form of a horrible skull. It seemed to move with a rotary motion and grin at him in a most frightful manner. Then he heard a loud, piercing laugh, and with that the skull vanished. The Highlander then rose from his chair, drew the dagger from his belt, and advanced towards the elder, who, his few remaining senses finally deserting him, fainted, and the following morning was thus found by the officer more dead than alive, and speedily conveyed to his home.

It was the custom in country places in those days for women to gather at a neighbour's house to ceilidh, and on this particular morning it so happened that a number were gathered in the elder's house. They saw the elder carried in and put to bed, then ran with all haste to spread the startling news. Among them was the shoemaker's wife, who ran to the shop to inform her husband. Rushing in excitedly, she shouted, "The elder is home, poor man, he was strangled by the ghost last night at the Castle!"

That was tragic news indeed for the poor shoemaker, whose turn it was to keep watch at the Castle that night. Dropping his work, he rose from the stool and stood speechless.

"What are you going to do?" his wife asked.

"What can I do but go," exclaimed the shoemaker. "I cannot refuse now."

"You will also be strangled by the ghost, and I will be a poor widow to-morrow," his wife wailed. "I hope you have the account book correct, or I will never be able to collect the debts from some of the people."

"It is money you are worrying about," said the shoemaker, "you do not consider my pitiful plight."

"It is your own bragging tongue that got you into this plight," answered his wife, "it has tied you in a knot this time that you won't loose easily with your teeth."

"Oh! I will have to bear the suffering," exclaimed the shoemaker, "but if I am murdered the fault lies at the minister's door, as he is to blame for forcing me to go."

"You offered yourself a willing sacrifice to please the Earl," said his wife.

"It surely amuses you to taunt me with your evil tongue," faltered the shoemaker. "Why do you excite me worse than I am?"

It was a miserable day for the shoemaker, but the night was worse. He arrived at the Castle, where the estate officer was waiting.

"Hurry up there," he shouted, as the shoemaker drew near, "I do not want to stay here all night."

The shoemaker followed him up the stairs until they came to the room, at the door of which the poor shoemaker hesitated.

"He sat down and the shoemaker was astounded to observe he had cloven hooves."

"Get into your 'chamber of horrors'," said the officer, giving him a violent push, and locking the door.

"Oh, don't lock me in here!" shouted the shoemaker. "Have mercy on me! I will go mad." He tried the door, but it was securely locked, then ran to the window, but there was no escape that way, for to drop meant certain death. He was now a prisoner in the haunted room, where he paced backwards and forwards for nearly an hour, a mass of nerves. At length he crept over and sat down in one of the chairs. Not a sound was to be heard in the Castle, and the stillness made him even more nervous. In an attempt to keep his courage up, he began singing psalms, and had just finished the line, "Therefore although the earth remove, we will not be afraid," when the door opened and a tall man entered. His shape and form suggested to the shoemaker that it was no other than the Devil. Advancing to the chair, he sat down, and the shoemaker was astounded to observe that he had cloven hooves. The man crossed one leg over the other until one of his hooves nearly touched the shoemaker's knee. At this, weakness overcame the shoemaker. Cold shivers ran down his spine, a haze came over his eyes, and he hoped it was death. Glancing round, he saw in the mirror near the fireplace the gruesome form of a skeleton grinning at him. Then, hearing a creaking noise at his side, he looked down and beheld a skeleton sitting on the edge of the table. It was this gruesome form he had seen reflected in the mirror.

At length the strange man in the chair bestirred himself and said "What seeketh thou here? Do you wish to join our company?"

The shoemaker, now in a state of abject terror, could make no answer, his breath coming in but painful gasps.

"Damn you, can you not answer a civil question?" cried the man angrily, at the same time giving him a violent push with his hoof.

The shoemaker saw the skeleton point a long, bony finger towards him, and heard it in a croaking voice say, "That's your man, away with him." With that the Devil sprang from his chair, as if to claim his victim, and the terror-stricken shoemaker collapsed in an unconscious condition, and thus he was found the following morning.

The fourth and last night Rob Angus kept watch. He arrived early and met the estate officer at the door.

"Hullo, Rob, you have arrived," said the officer.

"Aye, did you think I was afraid to come?" asked Rob.

"No, Rob, but I wish it was all over; what with all these unconscious madmen I get every morning, my own nerves are getting affected."

"You will get no unconscious madman to-morrow morning," said Rob. "You will either find me as I am, or dead."

"God forbid! don't speak like that, man," exclaimed the officer.

The ground officer and Rob were old friends, who had had many a spree together.

"Let us go up to the room, and have a taste of my own brewing," said Rob.

So they went upstairs, entered the room, and sat down in the easy chairs by the fire. Rob pulled a bottle from his pocket, handed it to his companion, and told him "to take a good drink." It was pure whisky, straight from the worm, and clear as water. Taking a copious draught from the bottle, and handing it to Rob, the officer remarked, "that is champion whisky, the like was never brewed."

"I can make a good drop whisky," replied Rob, "when I get peace from the gauger."

"You ought to have a big trade, with that quality of whisky," said the officer.

"More trade than I can supply," Rob made answer, "but I can only make it in small quantities, until I get a proper distillery. Perhaps the Earl will build one for me."

At that they both laughed and had another drink from the bottle. Rob, having that day finished loading a boat with spirits he had been brewing for several months, had been drinking fairly heavily, but , as he was accustomed to strong drink, it took a large quantity to affect him. The strong spirits were now showing their effects on the officer, who commenced singing, and vaunted his intention to remain with Rob for the night.

"Do you wish to get yourself into the same state as the elder and the shoemaker?" asked Rob, smiling.

31

"Oh! God forbid," said the officer. "The Lord only knows what made the minister select you weak-minded creatures."

"I can tell you that," said Rob. "Because he could not get any better. There's plenty brave enough to laugh at the Castle stories, but devilish frightened to stay a night in it."

"They would never have stayed the night if I did not lock them in," said the officer. "That is what drove them mad."

"They are surely not as bad as that?" said Rob.

"Aren't they?" replied his companion, "wait till you hear the whole story. The first morning I got the minister busy reading a book in that chair where you are sitting. I knew by his face that he had not seen anything out of the ordinary. But the next morning I found the elder unconscious. I really thought he was dead when I first went over to him. I had to get the men from the farm to help me carry him down the stairs and then we put him into a cart and took him home. The following morning I got the shoemaker in the same condition. It was awful to hear them raving about the sights they saw – enough to drive any ordinary man mad. I was present when Dr Crombie was questioning the shoemaker. He told the doctor in his delirium that he saw the Devil, with cloven hooves, sitting in a chair beside him, and kicking him when he would not answer his questions. He then raved about a skeleton, sitting on the table there, which asked the devil to take the shoemaker away. He also told the doctor that the devil caught him and crushed him in his grip, and that all his bones were broken, but the doctor cannot find a mark on him."

"What does the doctor think of it?" asked Rob.

"Dr Crombie is just laughing," replied his companion. "I know what he would like, aye, and would be willing to pay a handsome sum for too – their dead bodies! He would be in his element examining their brains. He would soon lay their brain-boxes open and start exploring through them for a mental kink, and think no more about it than you or me would of opening a cockle."

Rob laughed and remarked, "Well, you had better be going now; it is nearly half-past eleven. Have another dram before you go, and I will see you in the morning."

32

The officer helped himself, then, bidding Rob good-night, locked the door and rather unsteadily wended his way home.

He was the last man to see brave Rob Angus alive. On arriving at the Castle next morning he got a dreadful shock when, on opening the door of the haunted room, he found the whole place a wreck. The table and chairs were up-turned and broken, the beautiful mirror lay in a hundred pieces, pictures were smashed on the floor, but there was no sign of Rob Angus.

Looking towards the window he observed that it was gone, framework and all, and, hurrying forward, he was horrified to observe through the aperture the form of a man on the ground below. His worst forebodings were realised when, on running down the stairs and hastening round, he found that the body was that of poor Rob Angus.

CHAPTER IX

WHAT THE DROVER SAW

It was never known whether Rob leaped or was thrown out of the window, but a peculiar account of the occurrence was given by a veteran drover. On the night Rob went to the Castle the drover happened to be passing that way with a flock of sheep. He enquired of the farmer who owned the farm beside the Castle if he could get a place to rest his sheep and himself, as he had come a long distance that day and was very weary. The farmer, a kind-hearted man, told him to put the sheep in the field round the castle, and he himself could stay in the bothy with the ploughmen till morning. As packmen and drovers were the principal means of conveying news from one part to the other, they were generally made welcome in country places. They always possessed an interesting store of information about the different parts of the country where they journeyed. Drovers were generally a strong, hardy type of men, who could walk long distances, sometimes with very little food, and exposed to all kinds of weather. After partaking of a hearty supper, the drover sat down at the bothy fire, and told the farmer and his servants many interesting stories of his experiences on the road. When they asked how he managed to get a place of shelter for himself and his flock on some of his journeys they were shocked when he told them that he usually made for a graveyard, where he could keep his sheep together, and sleep himself wrapt in his plaid. If it was very cold or stormy he would crawl under one of the flat grave-stones, and lie there. He would be a brave man who would crawl under a gravestone and sleep for a night in a lonesome churchyard. But that many a drover had to do, and be very thankful for the slight shelter it afforded. They were undoubtedly a brave, hardy race of men.

About half-past twelve the ploughmen decided it was time for bed, so the drover got up and said he was going to take a turn round his sheep to see if they were all right. He was a stranger in the district, and knew nothing about the Castle or its history. There was a full moon, and everything was as clear as day. Passing the castle, he went round to the other side, where his sheep were resting. He observed a light in one of the windows, but thinking the Castle was occupied, he took no particular notice. However, as he drew nearer, he heard an awful noise, as if a violent struggle was taking place, followed by wild, shrill screams and angry shouts. He stood intently listening, then heard a noise like something heavy being knocked down, and the light suddenly went out. He kept a watch on the window, and, with the aid of the moon, he saw the form of a man being violently thrown out. He saw him fall, and heard the heavy thud as the body struck the ground. Then all was silent, and he was on the point of going over to investigate, when, happening to look towards the window, he saw a frightful sight, and took to his heels. Bounding into the bothy, he told what he had witnessed at the Castle, and the farm hands were greatly terrified. When asked later what he saw at the window which frightened him so much, he replied that it was the dreadful, hideous face of the Devil, with eyes sparkling like fire, and long, bright shining teeth, which was staring down at him.

"He kept watch on the window, and, with the aid of the moon, he saw the form of a man being violently thrown out."

Next morning, while the drovers and the others were at breakfast, the ground officer came hastily into the bothy, and excitedly told them that Rob Angus was dead, and asking for the use of a cart to have him brought home.

Then the drover gathered his sheep and took to the road.

35

That night the only one to meet the Earl was the minister, who found no solution to the strange mystery, except what was divulged to him in a dream. The incoherent accounts given by the elder and the shoemaker could hardly be credited, owing to their confused state of mind, and Rob Angus was dead.

No further effort was ever made to solve the mystery of Castle Stuart, and to this day it holds within its grim walls the ghostly secret.

John Cameron,
Ardesier,
March 1930

Epilogue

John Cameron was a well known Highland Games athlete. He made no pretence at being a writer; he simply wished to tell the tale of Castle Stuart as it had been related to him. Proceeds from the sale of this book will fund a prize in his name for future Highland Games.

Printed by A4 Print, Inverness